CREATING HOMES THAT
SUSTAIN OUR LIVES,
ECONOMY, AND THE EARTH

CREATING HOMES THAT SUSTAIN OUR LIVES, ECONOMY, AND THE EARTH

DR. JOHN H. FITCH

Library of Congress Control Number:		2020904257
ISBN:	Hardcover	978-1-7960-9120-5
	Softcover	978-1-7960-9119-9
	eBook	978-1-7960-9118-2

Printed in the United States of America

Rev. date: 04/20/2020

To order additional copies of this book, contact:
Xlibris
1-888-795-4274
www.Xlibris.com
Orders@Xlibris.com
804627

CONTENTS

DEDICATION

THE BOOK IS dedicated to former President Jimmy Carter for his ongoing support of sustainability and renewable energy, and to the far-sighted leaders and voters of California for supporting a solar energy mandate for all new homes.

In 1979, President Jimmy Carter had the courage and fortitude to install solar panels on the White House and to champion the promise of sustainability and renewable energy worldwide. At the dedication of the solar panels, he said:

> In the year 2000, this solar water heater behind me which is being dedicated today, will still be supplying cheap, efficient energy...A generation from now, this solar heater can either be a curiosity, a museum piece, an example of a road not taken, or it can be just a small part of one of the greatest and most exciting adventures ever undertaken by the American people.

In retirement, President Carter has continued to advance that cause as a volunteer with Habitat for Humanity and as an outspoken advocate for sustainability and renewable resources. At the age of 96, he and Rosalynn have given the village of Plains, Georgia an incredible gift! They leased 10 acres of land near their home and, working with SolAmerica, built a 1.3-megawatt solar farm that will supply more than 55 million kilowatt hours of renewable solar energy annually to the citizens of Plains, more than half of the town's total annual electricity consumption! The Carters truly personify the challenge of being the change that they wish to see in the world.

In 2019, the many individuals, villages, and elected leaders in California supported state legislation requiring mandatory solar panel installations on all new homes that are not shaded from the sun. In an interview with the *Mercury News*, California Energy Commissioner Kent Sasaki said, "This is the beginning of a substantial improvement in how we produce energy and reduce the consumption of fossil fuels." This legislation will provide a useful model for other states who see the strategic as well as the economic advantages of renewable energy production.

Sometimes it takes a village to raise a person who then becomes a catalyst for future change that greatly improves the world. In other cases, the village becomes the catalyst. I dedicate this book to two catalysts—Jimmy Carter and the State of California—who have courageously advanced sustainable building and the use of renewable energy resources.

Professor Brian Dunbar, LEED Fellow

A S EXECUTIVE DIRECTOR of the Institute for the Built Environment and Professor Emeritus of Construction Management at Colorado State University, I am honored to write the Foreword for *Creating Homes That Sustain Our Lives, Economy, and the Earth* by Dr. John Fitch.

I have known John for more than a decade and have been impressed with his work as an active scientist and leader conducting research, teaching, and helping to develop policies in the areas of ecosystems conservation, wildlife ecology, and sustainability. His slogan is "sustaining tomorrow today," and he believes in working to integrate economic, environmental, and societal planning and development for a sustainable future. His work has reflected his belief that he and his students should work on government and community levels as well as on academic pursuits. For example, he has worked as a Fellow in the Carter Administration on sustainability and wildlife conservation. John held appointments on the Tufts University faculty and as chief scientist for the Massachusetts Audubon Society and also directed publication of *"The Energy Saver's Handbook for Town and City People"* published by Rodale Press.

Although Dr. Fitch is not an architect or engineer, he has had a real passion for sustainable housing. While at Florida Gulf Coast University, he and his students worked with the city of Bonita Springs on an EPA grant to develop Southwest Florida's first affordable sustainable housing project. Dr. Fitch and his students were invited by EPA in 2002 to exhibit their designs on the Washington Mall during Earth Day festivities. Subsequently, Dr. Fitch decided to take a "sustainable home prospecting vacation" through the Rocky Mountains to find a place where he could relocate, build, and live in a sustainable demonstration home. I was pleased John selected the Fort Collins, Colorado area in which to build his home.

I gladly incorporated John's project into a graduate course in sustainable technology at Colorado State University. John joined me in providing guidance to the twenty construction, design, and engineering students, each of whom subsequently performed specific green design and construction research. The final report the students developed, more than 100 pages in length, provided in-depth meaningful research and recommendations for optimizing the home's performance while minimizing its environmental impacts. During the latter part of the course, students interviewed prospective builders; their reviews were quite helpful in selecting a builder who was especially interested in building a sustainable demonstration home.

Dr. Fitch then applied many of the sustainable aspects identified by students in directing the building of his sustainable home. He worked with the builder and subs to develop a creative team that could use sustainable strategies to full advantage as the home was being built. Construction on his home began in September of 2006 and was completed on July 7, 2007. In the 12 years since his home was completed, he has welcomed more than 600 visitors including students, the general public, and energy experts from four different countries. He also has had opportunities to monitor his home in terms of energy use, solar energy production, and dependability. Blower door tests by Poudre Valley Rural Electric Association (PVREA) confirmed that the home was the tightest one they had ever tested. Because Dr. Fitch's solar electric cells produce more power than he needs, he is able to sell power back to PVREA.

I encouraged Dr. Fitch to describe his impressive sustainable home and report on the tremendous advantages that such a home can provide for people—whether they live in rural areas, suburban neighborhoods or cities and whether they live in houses, apartments, or condos. I hope you will find this book helpful as a guide to remodel your current residence or build a sustainable home, one that can significantly reduce your utility bills and improve indoor air quality. An additional benefit is knowing that you are saving money as well as creating both a healthier indoor environment and a healthier planet as you use renewable resources!

As I look back at the process—John's original dream and site searching, the integration of the project into a graduate course, our students earnestly conducting research and developing design ideas that aligned with the overall vision and the successful construction experience—I am constantly amazed. This is a unique, compelling, and important story that I sincerely hope propels others to contribute to a healthier lifestyle and planet, just as John has done.

PROLOGUE

I N LATE NOVEMBER of 2019 there was an early winter storm that dumped four feet of snow in Redstone Canyon, above Fort Collins and Loveland, Colorado. I awoke that morning to the sound of a strong blizzard outdoors with high winds and snow lashing my home. I checked the output from my weather station and discovered winds of 45 mph and an outdoor temperature of 5 degrees F. Inside my home, the temperature was a comfortable 73 degrees F. I discovered through email that the electric grid in the canyon had been down for at least six hours because a tree had fallen on electric lines along the road in the lower canyon. I decided to have breakfast and plugged in my coffee maker before beginning to clear my driveway of the 4 feet of snow that had fallen.

You, the reader, are likely to have several questions about my statements above and let me try to guess some of them. First, if the electric grid power has been off for six hours with an outdoor temperature of 5 degrees F, how could the indoor temperature of my home still be at a comfortable 73 degrees F? Another question might be, that if the grid power was off, why was I turning on my electric coffee maker? Third, you might ask: Where can I return this book for a refund?

After a nice hot breakfast, I suited up in warm clothing as the storm slackened and used my electric leaf blower to blow snow away from the garage doors so that I could clear snow around the house and driveway with my electric snow blower and my Polaris Ranger ATV equipped with a plow. I should mention, as a hint, that my Polaris Ranger ATV is not gas-powered.

You certainly deserve some answers about the above statements. First, although my house is connected to the Poudre Valley Rural Electric Association (RVREA) grid, I also have solar panels collecting electric power, and a battery system storing electricity over and above what I use, either to be sold back to the grid or to be used if the grid goes down. Second, I have a solar hot water system mounted on my roof that supplies radiant heat by warming the floors in my home, with a back-up hot-water vault if the roof solar panels are covered with snow. In addition, the walls and ceiling of my home are super-insulated, so much of the heat generated stays within the house. Third, my electric leaf and snow blower as well as my Ranger Polaris ATV run on lithium batteries recharged by the energy produced from my solar panels.

I congratulate your patience if you are still reading, because you are about to discover what sustainable homes are and how they work. Sustainable homes, including mine, have several important characteristics that I will mention briefly now and discuss in more detail later. First, sustainable homes are positioned for maximum exposure to the sun; second, they are very well insulated; third, they make full use of renewable energy resources such as the sun and/or wind; fourth, they can store renewable energy through batteries for times when sun and/or wind renewable energies are low or not being produced, and fifth, they can either be independent from electric grids and store energy on site through battery storage, or they can be electric grid-connected to use grid energy at times when renewable energies such as sunlight are not being produced.

For reasons that you will discover in this book, sustainable building approaches can be used for almost any type of building including apartments, condos, homes, schools, and commercial buildings. Sustainable buildings represent a change in building design every bit as revolutionary as moving from log cabins to stick-built buildings. Sustainable buildings also represent new opportunities for the use of readily available renewable energies such as solar and wind while avoiding the damaging impacts of non-renewable fossil fuels upon air and water quality as well as long-term climate changes. Sustainable buildings have a tremendous advantage over conventional buildings in that they can use renewable energy from sun and wind that is readily available without requiring the great economic and environmental expenses of extracting that energy from the Earth.

My purposes in writing this book are first to introduce the tremendous advantages of sustainable building, especially for the residential homes of town and country people; second, to suggest how people without construction and building skills can select good building sites, skilled and reliable architects, engineers, capable builders, and knowledgeable loan officers; and third, to encourage more architects, engineers, loan officers, builders, and suppliers to become a part of the growing sustainable building infrastructure.

When I first heard about sustainable homes, I thought the information on energy and financial savings was too good to be true. That changed when I reviewed some of the energy and economic data coming out of sustainable homes. Next, I wondered about construction costs as well as superinsulation and renewable energy technology costs. Isn't it much more expensive to construct a sustainable home with superinsulation and renewable energy solar panels and control systems? However, I discovered that forced hot-air furnaces and ducting were not needed, accounting for considerable savings. In addition, renewable energy systems, including solar panels and related equipment, were less expensive due to federal and state tax incentives.

After some years of growing familiarity with sustainable buildings through public policy and environmental teaching and research, I decided to build a sustainable demonstration home in which I would live and about which I could give tours and teach with direct experience.

To date, more than 600 people, including energy experts from four different countries, have visited my sustainable home, and I have excellent information on not only the effectiveness of the technology and the practicality of using renewable energy, but also on the tremendous savings in monthly utility costs. In addition, when considering the tax incentives of sustainable energy collecting and efficiency technologies, my sustainable home cost no more to build than a conventional home!

My experience of having a sustainable home built and then living in it has been so positive that I decided to write a book about the building process and the experience in living in a sustainable home as a way of celebrating the 50th anniversary of Earth Day and helping others to appreciate the possibilities for sustainable homes in the future!

I believe that these purposes can best be achieved by sharing my experiences in planning and having built my own sustainable home. After much advice, planning, and working with good people, I was able to test and verify that my sustainable home cost no more to build than a conventional home, with monthly utility costs of less than 10% of what a conventional home in the same region would experience!

I should mention up front that I personally lack the construction and building skills to build any type of house. I am a left-hander, and most tools, power and otherwise, are designed for right-handed people. I would rather capture live rattlesnakes or study bears and mountain lions than redo a bathroom! Please realize that if I have had a hand in designing a sustainable home and have been able to navigate the ways of building a sustainable home, you can, too. And there is another benefit: it has been one of the great challenges and experiences of my life that keeps on giving even after the sustainable home has been completed. Being able to live in a sustainable home is a wonderful experience and knowing that it is energized by readily available and non-polluting renewable energy with significant economic savings makes the experience even better!

Another purpose in writing this book is to provide information on how to go about arranging to have a sustainable house built. There are already a number of books available for gifted "do-it-yourselfers," and I will mention them in passing. However, the main points of emphasis of this book, assuming that you have about the same building skills as I do, are: 1) what sustainable features are important to have in a sustainable home, 2) how might those sustainable features be integrated to provide power in emergencies, 3) how do you select an appropriate building site, 4) how do you find a reliable architect, engineer, and builder, 5) what are some challenges in obtaining financing for your home, and 6) what concerns should you have in insuring and protecting your sustainable home investment.

Specifically, I will first introduce the tremendous advantages of sustainable building, especially for the residential homes of town and country people. I will then suggest how people without construction and building skills can select good building sites, skilled and reliable architects, engineers, and builders, and knowledgeable loan officers. Finally, I will encourage more architects, engineers, loan officers, builders, and suppliers to become a part of the growing sustainable building infrastructure.

INTRODUCTION

WOULD YOU LIKE to live in a comfortable, well-insulated sustainable home that costs no more to build than a conventional home? Would you like this home to be capable of providing its own heating and cooling systems with utilities bills of less than 10% per month compared to what they would cost in a conventional home? Would you like the energy used for heating, cooling, lighting, and cooking to be from renewable sources such as the sun and/or wind that are available right on your property? Would you like to be able to sell your unused power back to the electric grid? Would you like to know that the comfortable, sustainable home in which you are living is helping to sustain your budget? And, finally, would you like to know that your home is also helping to sustain the Earth by using non-polluting renewable energy sources and building materials? If you answer "yes" to even one of these questions, you should read this book.

I know this sounds too good to be true. That is exactly how I felt when I first became interested in sustainable homes. As a scientist, I am by no means a person with the skills necessary to build such a home. But as I discovered more about sustainable homes and their advantages, I decided I had to try having a sustainable home built for myself. I also learned you can build sustainably no matter whether you are in town, in suburbia, or in a rural area.

I am writing this book for several audiences. First, if you are interested in any or all of the benefits of sustainable homes, this book is definitely for you. It will give you information on available sustainable technologies; how to select an appropriate area in which to build and a site in that area that would be good for building; how to select a good architect, a knowledgeable engineer, and a reliable sustainable builder and crew; how to obtain financing; how to work with inspectors; and how to integrate different sustainable technologies and equipment into the home.

This book will also be helpful to people who are considering getting involved in the growing infrastructure of sustainable architects, engineers, builders, building suppliers, computer engineers, and landscape experts. These experts are creating the foundation for a sustainable construction industry. This is a new, exciting, and expanding cooperative of experts who enjoy innovative and challenging opportunities.

Finally, sustainability provides new opportunities for do-it-yourselfers as well. People who are handy and who relish the challenge of building a sustainable home will find this book and its reference section very helpful. An important element of sustainable home design is the successful integration of different systems for maximum productivity. For example, people caught in the severe fires in California discovered their garage doors would not open when the power grid was shut down. If they lived in sustainable homes with solar energy backup, they would have been able to operate their garage doors, refrigerators, air conditioners, water heaters, and well pumps without difficulty even if the electric grid was down.

I decided to write this book at this time because we live in an increasingly complex world with continuous change and growing challenges. In such times, if we concentrate on finding solutions that are at once helpful to us personally, beneficial to our long-term economy, and of benefit to the Earth, we cannot go wrong. That is the litmus test I apply in these complicated times.

Skeptics of sustainability argue that such advantages and benefits might be theoretically possible but ask for proof that they have actually been achieved for people in real life. This is an important point because, as we have all discovered, the theoretically possible is not necessarily achievable. I am pleased to report that after twelve years of living in and monitoring my sustainable demonstration home I have been able to achieve all of these benefits and more!

I chose 2020, the 50th anniversary of Earth Day, as the time to release this book for good reason. Sustainable building and renewable energy have come of age and are now practical and affordable. This year is the 50th anniversary of the first Earth Day which was held on April 22, 1970. In the aftermath of the Vietnam War, this nation gathered and worked together as bipartisan Americans to pass major legislation that addressed the environmental problems of the time. With the "2020" vision for our new decade, let us work together to "sustain tomorrow today" by moving toward a sustainable building future that will benefit us, our economy, and the Earth that supports us!

On a personal note, it is difficult for me to put into words the superb quality of health and life I enjoy living in my sustainable home in Redstone Canyon, only 15 minutes from beautiful Horsetooth Reservoir and only 20 more minutes to Fort Collins. If only everyone could live in a progressive city like Fort Collins that has pledged to be using 100% renewable energy by the year 2030!

CHAPTER 1

Planning And Building My
Rural Sustainable Home

WHAT IS A sustainable home? First, it is a home that is carefully located to fit with the site topography in such a way as to minimize environmental damage. Second, it is oriented with a good southern exposure to enable solar hot water heating and also for photovoltaic energy production. Third, the home is super-insulated to reduce both heating and cooling requirements. Fourth, it is significantly powered by renewable energy from the sun. Fifth, the home is built with durable and non-toxic materials that can be recycled in the future. Sixth, although I never contemplate getting old, the home is planned with universal design features such as a mechanical dumbwaiter between floors. Seventh, the carefully selected building materials reduce site construction waste to less than 10% of what conventional home construction would add to the waste stream. Last, regenerative efforts are made to restore native vegetation to the construction site.

My sustainable home with solar panels nestled into
Redstone Canyon near Fort Collins, Colorado

I cannot over emphasize the importance of planning in the building of any home, especially a sustainable one. Setting off on a vacation to climb a mountain or explore a cave, you would certainly develop a plan based on three major considerations: your goals for the trip, the actions you will need to accomplish, and the equipment you must take to be safe and successful.

Likewise, in planning a sustainable home, you will have many choices to make. You will have to consider many elements you wish to have in your sustainable home and select reliable and knowledgeable people for its construction. In this chapter, I illustrate these planning steps with examples from my own experience in having built and lived in a sustainable home. Below I have organized most if not all of these considerations into seven steps. In Chapter 2, I report on the outcomes of the decisions I made for my own home.

Step #1: Seeking a Context and Place for My Sustainable Home

How does one envision a personal sustainable future? Reflection is a good first step in the process of planning a home. Having enjoyed a rich and rewarding professional life, and at the age of 64, I decided in 2008 that it was time for me to seek a unique place where I could build a sustainable home, affiliate with a good university, teach and write as a senior faculty member, and be relatively unfettered by the politics and bureaucracy of complex institutions!

After some envisioning exercises, I decided I would like to build a sustainable home on wildland property somewhere in the Rocky Mountains area. That decision gave me a wonderful excuse in the summer of 2008 to take a "prospecting vacation", beginning in Silver City, New Mexico and following the Rocky Mountains all the way up to Glacier National Park. I selected several stops along the way for some land-prospecting with Realtors and evaluated other important factors such as the character and sustainable infrastructure of nearby towns, higher education opportunities and medical facilities, and proximity to nearby areas of ecological interest. My dream was to find a place where I could build a sustainable demonstration home on some private wildlands, close enough to an academic institution so I could combine building the home with ecological research and teaching. Ideally, I wanted to find a region where I could experience the natural environment, interesting history, arts, music, and outdoor activities (kayaking, nature study, photography, cross-country skiing, exploring, etc.) as well as a place to grow old as gracefully as possible.

One of the places I especially wanted to visit was the Fort Collins, Colorado area. It is known for Colorado State University with its strengths in the academic areas of sustainability, ecological/wildlands, and wildlife research. I arrived in Fort Collins one afternoon, bought a picnic dinner at a local grocery and went to Horsetooth Reservoir to eat my supper. Because I am a dedicated kayaker, I was very excited about the prospect of kayaking in such a beautiful place. As skies brightened with a magnificent sunset, I was amazed at the beauty of the sunlight reflecting on the red sandstone boulders in some places and the gray granite outcropping in others. It was no surprise that this place had been given the name of Redstone Canyon!

Southwest side of iconic Horsetooth Rock near Fort Collins, Colorado

The vegetation along County Road 25 E alternates between creek-bottom cottonwoods and willows to prairie grassland in higher areas and ponderosa pine in still higher elevations. The Canyon is two or three miles wide at its base and is approximately 9 miles long as it narrows to a half-mile in width at its upper end. Redstone Canyon Creek intermittently flows the length of the canyon to over 7,300 feet on the ridge tops, affording wonderful views of dramatic features like Hosetooth Rock.

The next day, I had a meeting with a land Realtor, Al Hamilton, and I raved about Redstone Canyon. He laughed and said that given my interests, he was going to tell me first about Redstone Canyon and, furthermore, that he lived up there for the same reasons! As we discussed the canyon, I came to realize that although it was only 45 minutes from Fort Collins, through a combination of fortuitous circumstances, it is a place that has been able to sustain its wildness as well as to offer its private landowners an amazing quality of life. As a conservationist who has worked extensively on conservation issues, I was intrigued with the land use history of Redstone Canyon.

Redstone Canyon was originally owned by two ranches. In the mid-1950s, they fell on hard times and had to be sold. At about the same time, the Colorado legislature passed laws allowing rural homeowner associations to require up to 30 acres per house in an effort to conserve ecological and geological gems like Redstone Canyon. The Swanson Cattle Ranch land was gradually acquired by Ken Reese and Don Clarke, a conservation-minded Denver attorney, who were with Clinton Realty and Swanson Associates. Because of their work, on May 14, 1979, the Redstone Canyon Corporation was officially certified by the Colorado Department of State as a nonprofit corporation operating under the name of Redstone Canyon Association. This association required the minimum 30 acres per house to conserve natural lands and maintain existing natural ecosystems. As a result, the ridges of Redstone Canyon have supported wildlife diversity and the relatively undisturbed movement of large mammals including elk, deer, black bears, mountain sheep, and mountain lions between Rocky Mountain National Park and Redstone Canyon. Colorado state parks and Larimer County parks along the Horsetooth Reservoir have continued to support and enhance the movement of wildlife in the area. Recently, Larimer County along with the City of Fort Collins purchased easements along the ridge tops to protect them from development.

South facing slopes of Redstone Canyon

Although I had worked on a variety of other land conservation initiatives with The Nature Conservancy in other states, I was attracted to this innovative approach to conservation that spaced homes far apart rather than clustering them in a central place. I was intrigued by the question of which might be the most effective conservation model—allowing large lots and expecting good stewardship from homeowners, or clustering houses that were surrounded by the conservation land.

I soon learned that Redstone Canyon had several other state-of-the-art conservation practices. One was to allow limited cattle grazing that was carefully monitored by a grazing specialist at CSU, in order to maintain the Canyon's mixed pine and prairie grasslands and to reduce forest and grassland fire fuel. Another was to allow participating landowners to claim agricultural exemptions. Because of the annual cattle leases and exemptions, association fees could be kept low while still providing the Redstone Canyon Association with funds to maintain association roads.

After checking on other properties in this area as well as continuing my travels up to Glacier National Park, I became convinced that Redstone Canyon was the place to be with its proximity to Fort Collins and CSU as well as the intriguing conservation methods that made it a very attractive option for a sustainable demonstration home site. In addition, the Canyon was only 20 minutes from boat launching facilities at Horsetooth Reservoir. Don Clarke was very supportive of my plans and ended up selling me a beautiful piece of property measuring 30 acres as the crow flies. Because it is on the south side of the Canyon, it is an excellent piece of land with both native grassland interspersed with ponderosa pine forests. I have recorded mountain lions, eagles, elk, bears, mule deer, and coyotes on my land which is a wonderful experience for an ecologist.

House site showing proximity to association road

Step # 2: Envisioning the Critical Elements of My Sustainable Home

Having decided that Fort Collins, Colorado State University, and Redstone Canyon would be an ideal area in which to live and work, the next step was very challenging for me. With only enough knowledge about sustainable homes to make me dangerous, and with a desire to make this process a learning experience for me and others, how best could I proceed?

Professor Brian Dunbar, who was also kind enough to write the Foreword to this book, suggested a wonderful option. Brian has a national reputation as a sustainable architect and is a Green Building Fellow with the national U.S. Green Building Council. We had worked before on ideas for the first low-income affordable and sustainable housing project in Southwest Florida.

Brian was scheduled to teach a course in sustainable home design for graduate architecture students and suggested I co-teach the course with him, using my sustainable home as the planning project for the class! During the semester we studied sustainability in home construction in all its aspects, from planning to design to construction. During the latter part of the class term, we even brought in prospective building contractors to discuss their backgrounds and recommendations for a high-performance sustainable home. This was a new experience for several of the contractors but a great way of sorting out possibilities for both the students and me.

By the end of the term, the class had developed a comprehensive, 200-page report entitled *The Fitch Residence High-Performance Design and Sustainable Development Recommendations: A Student Report.* This document, as well as the excellent class discussions, gave me the information I needed to develop major priorities for my sustainable home and, most importantly, the plans for integrating the different systems to optimize both performance and reliability.

As a result of the class and of envisioning the home I wanted to build, I was able to decide on the most critical elements I would pursue. I would have built a high-performance sustainable house that would use structurally insulated panels to provide both strength and high insulation levels in the walls. In addition, it would have spray foam insulation in the ceilings of from three to four times the insulative values of those of conventional homes. The home would have a good southern exposure with solar hot-water panels mounted on the south-facing roof to heat water for the radiant floor heating system. Very sturdy south-facing windows would provide solar heat during the winter months, but the configuration of this two-story home with an upper deck would allow shading those windows from the summer sun. A special film on the inside of glass windows and doors would absorb the solar heat when it is at a more direct angle (as in the winter) and reflect it when at an oblique angle (as in the summer). The windows and sliding glass doors would also have double-pane glass throughout, affording excellent views in all directions.

The land near the home would have additional mounted photovoltaic solar panels to produce 10% to 15% more electrical power than the home would need that could then be sold back to Poudre Valley Rural Electric Association. I would also have a battery backup system for powering my sustainable home if the grid went down.

These were all preliminary decisions. The next step was to select a building contractor with sustainable building interest and experience and a crew to build my sustainable home. I needed to find a contractor who was trustworthy, well-organized, knowledgeable about and committed to sustainable building, and very honest in projecting costs and providing documentation. At the same time, I had to select and purchase a good building site in Redstone Canyon!

Step #3: Selecting a Reliable and Knowledgeable Contractor

Initially, I considered a hybrid sustainable home that had timber framing. I found a contractor who said he had experience in bringing together the aspects of timber framing and superinsulation. However, his performance with students in the class raised some questions in my mind about his commitment and knowledge of integrating superinsulation and timber-framing design as well as his commitment to coming in on budget. To test my concerns, I paid him to create a detailed plan and budget proposal. In our class discussion of his plan, it became apparent that he did not appreciate the need for superinsulation, nor was he able to defend his budget and cost estimates. He finally said that the project might cost 20% more than projected, but I would have a really nice home. I thanked him and went on to the next potential contractor.

This contractor had won awards for sustainable homes, did well with student questions, produced a well-documented budget, and had contacts with some excellent carpenters, electricians, and suppliers of insulated panels, solar electric and hot water panels, as well as installers. I checked with his references concerning his ability to stay on or close to established budgets. In addition, my goal was to develop an interacting construction team rather than a group of individual subcontractors who simply did specialized work but did not coordinate and innovate with the other participants. The contractor I selected seemed very supportive of this approach.

Step #4: Selecting a Good and Affordable Building Site

The challenges of selecting a good building site in a beautiful and semi-wild canyon were unique and fun. Redstone Canyon is a very special place because of its geological and biological beauty and diversity. Elk, black bears, mule deer, mountain lions, coyote, and mink include Redstone Canyon in their home ranges and seasonal travels. As an ecologist, I decided that these are all very positive reasons to live there. The canyon is on the west side of Horsetooth Rock and varies in elevation ranging from 4,200 feet at the mouth of Redstone Canyon to 7,300 feet at the top of the highest ridge. A county gravel road traverses the first seven miles of the canyon and maintenance and snow removal for that road are provided by Larimer County.

Upon my return trip through Redstone Canyon, I put in a bid on a piece of land in the bottom of the Canyon but was outbid by someone offering cash. It was just as well.

In my research on Redstone Canyon, I became acquainted with the above-mentioned attorney who started the Redstone Canyon Homeowner's Association as well as the Realtor who lives in the canyon. I was looking for a saddleback, a hillside where the soil and smaller rocks have accumulated to make an almost level area. When I could not find the right combination of a south-facing slope with a fairly level saddleback area, the attorney and Realtor worked out a solution. I was offered 30 acres of the attorney's own personal property which, if this hillside were flattened, would be closer to 55 acres. Not only did this property have a view of Rocky Mountain National Park, but also of Pikes Peak, more than 200 miles to the south. It was on a parcel with an association road and powerline easement going through the property and a level saddleback area for a home fairly close to the road. The price was reasonable, and the attorney even offered to finance the purchase until I could get the home built. This offer turned out to be a wonderful one and just what I needed.

Having the association road going through the property gave me super access to the construction site, and I was able to put in a level access road to the area where my home would be built on an otherwise fairly vertical area. The saddleback area had wonderful sun exposure and an incredible view of the Redstone Canyon all the way down to Loveland. Another benefit was that power poles had already been installed along the association road, which went up to the top of the ridge. At a reported installation cost of $10,000 per pole, that represented quite a savings, because I could then be grid-connected and could sell power back to the grid. Since one pole on the association road was quite close to the house site, we received permission from the utility to run a line from the pole underneath the road to the house site, which was only about 200 yards away.

Ponderosa forest view from my deck looking southwest
toward Never Summer Mountain Range

Examination of the soil of the saddleback house site indicated it was composed of small rocks and soils that would require no blasting, and the soil was sufficiently loose so trenches could be dug with a backhoe for the foundation. Further, there was sufficient soil to establish a sewage disposal field. However, there was one additional serious issue. On the saddleback with the elevation of 6,600 feet, would I be able to drill a well that would strike water, and would that water be drinkable.? This was a question we had to answer before the house could be built. I was able to find an excellent well driller who was familiar with Redstone Canyon and had not only a master's degree in geology but was also a "water witcher," which covered both options! On the first try, the drilling produced a deep well with excellent production and water quality so good that no filtration has been necessary.

Finally, the building site was selected because it is in a grassland area with a number of trees. Several trees had to be cut or trimmed so the area in the vicinity of the house would be protected from fire. In addition, the house was planned to have a concrete apron around it to protect it from fire and the native grass on the immediate yard area was to be kept trimmed during the growing season.

Step # 5: Seeking Financing for My Sustainable Demonstration Home

After the above successes, I decided to seek a loan for my sustainable demonstration home from a local bank which shall remain nameless. Initially, the bank's vice president was very happy to see me, but his face fell when I started describing my sustainable demonstration home. He finally interrupted and said he had no idea of what I was talking about and that the bank would have to hire an engineer at my expense just to see whether my idea was viable and to demonstrate their due diligence! He told me they would love to lend me funding if I would only build a "real conventional" home. I wished him well and found a way of self-financing my sustainable home. Since then, I have discovered other non-local banks in Fort Collins that lend routinely on sustainable home projects.

Step #6: Pre-Construction Celebration of the Land

Prior to beginning the construction, it seemed important to have a celebration of the land, the geology, and the native peoples, plants, and animals that had lived or were presently living there. About 40 people, including neighbors to be, university faculty, and students, and a Ute representative attended the celebration of the land. At one point, we all formed a large circle and shared the following Native American prayer:

Great Spirit Prayer

Oh Great Spirit,
Whose voice I hear in the winds
and whose breath gives life to all the world.
Hear me! I need your strength and wisdom.
Let me walk in beauty, and make my eyes
ever hold the red and purple sunset.
Make my hands respect the things you have made
and my ears sharp to hear your voice.
Make me wise so that I may understand
the things you have taught my people.
Let me learn the lessons you have hidden
in every leaf and rock.

Help me remain calm and strong in the

face of all that comes towards me.
Help me find compassion without
empathy overwhelming me.
I seek strength, not to be greater than my brother,
but to fight my greatest enemy: myself.
Make me always ready to some to you
with clean hands and straight eyes.
So when life fades, as the facing sunset,
my spirit may come to you without shame.

- Translated by Lakota Sioux Chief Yellow Lark in 1887

Step #7: Preparing the Land for Construction

The celebration of the land and the discussions of how my sustainable home would fit and become a part of the land was a wonderful time. As part of the discussion, we decided that before the land was excavated for the foundation and sewage disposal field, the native grass would be rolled up and stored nearby and then unrolled as soon as the excavation was completed and the ground refilled. Rain barrels would be used initially to water the grass after the holes were refilled so no new grass had to be planted. There was much excitement that my home would be open to visitors such as grade school, high school, and university students as well as interested residents as soon as it was completed.

Step #8: Interior Layout

As we put together the plan, I was determined that we demonstrate ways in which sustainable systems could be integrated to reinforce one another and work together. We decided that the house should be approximately 2,300 square feet and have two stories. The first floor would have a walk-out basement with a bedroom/office, storage closets, a full bath, an equipment room, and a four-car garage with two garage doors. A second floor would include two bedroom/offices, two full baths, two walk-in closets, a kitchen/dining room, a living room, and a laundry room.

Step #9: Restoring the Home Building Site

The restoration of my sustainable home building site would be quite simple. The septic drain field was to be excavated in the saddleback after the native grass on the surface was rolled up much like turf, and then unrolled again once the drain field was installed. Along the driveway, rolled straw wattles were to be used to control erosion until native vegetation regrew and stabilized these areas. In areas of the driveway where the cut was more than four feet into the hill, recycled railroad ties were used to stabilize the hillside.

Step #10: Assessing the Economic Side of Building a Sustainable Home

We use two separate economic yardsticks to compare the total costs of building and living in a sustainable home versus a conventional home. As in deciding on the purpose of a car, one measure is the sticker price which includes the costs of the model's development, parts and their assembly, labor, and overhead. The second measure includes operative costs once the vehicle is purchased such as gas, maintenance, license plates, and other associated costs. The sticker price of home construction includes the costs of architectural plans and engineering analyses, permit application, research on building materials and their purchase, the price of the construction site, labor, clean-up, disposal of construction waste, and restoring the building site. The sticker price of conventional and sustainable home construction can be similar. But here the comparison diverges. Because the operating costs of sustainable homes are much less than for conventional homes, the *total* cost of sustainable home ownership is significantly less than living in a conventional home and that disparity becomes greater over time.

As an example, my sustainable home of 2,300 square feet cost $460,000 to construct in 2008. My utility/operating costs have averaged $40 per month or approximately $480 per year, or $14,400 over 30 years. In contrast, a conventionally built mountain home of the same size costing about the same to construct, may well average $400 per month in utility expenses or $144,000 over 30 years. A savings of $129,600 is not a bad return on my investment!

CHAPTER 2

Sustainable Features Of My
Home And Property

HAVING DISCUSSED THE planning process for designing a sustainable home in Chapter 1, here I describe the characteristics and features of my sustainable rural home and property and how they work together. Succinctly, my home meets the goals I established during its planning process. A sustainable home should be:

- Superinsulated to reduce both heating and cooling needs.
- Powered by renewable energy, especially solar energy, and perhaps wind, although if the wind blows too much or too little it will impact the home's insulative ability.
- Oriented on the site to take full advantage of renewable energy resources, and built with durable and nontoxic materials that can be recycled in the future.
- Constructed with universal design features allowing the home to be repurposed over time as conditions for the occupant(s) change.
- Located on the land to fit with the site topography in such a way as to minimize environmental damage to the land and its plants and animals
- Constructed with building materials selected to limit on-site construction waste to no more than 10% of the waste that is generated by nonsustainable home construction.

Restoration of my building site's front yard with native grass species

In this brief overview, I describe some of the major sustainable and regenerative choices I made when constructing my home in beautiful Redstone Canyon above Fort Collins. More difficult to describe is the great sense of health, closeness to nature, and the feeling of empowerment that comes naturally from living in a sustainable home! The purpose of this chapter is to share ideas that you can use in planning your own sustainable home, whether it is in the wilderness, in a rural development, or in a city. If you contemplate building, you might use the following as a checklist.

Exterior Sustainable Choices

Home Site Location. My home site is located on a grassland saddleback midway up the south-facing side of Redstone Canyon in Larimer County, Colorado at an altitude of 6,600 feet. A saddleback is a part of the hillside where soil and smaller rocks have accumulated to make an almost level area. By selecting this somewhat flat area without large rocks, no blasting was required in excavating and building the foundation. The parcel on which my home is located includes 30 acres on the side of the canyon and bisected by a Redstone Canyon Association (RCA) access road going through my property. The RCA access road continues up to the top of the canyon at an elevation of 7,200 feet where neighbors own several homes. Below my home, the association road connects with County Road 25E (maintained by Larimer County) at the bottom of the canyon providing access to a paved highway leading past Horsetooth Reservoir to Fort Collins. During the winter, residents are responsible for snow removal on association roads, so it is a good strategy to live below someone who enjoys snow plowing and has the equipment for snow removal.

The flatter saddleback location of my home site reduced construction disturbance to the hillside, allowed for optimal drainage, and provided a stable substrate for the house foundation. Nearby forests to the west of the house provide some protection from storms and high winds even after being thinned for fire mitigation and protection. The house site has a relatively short and level driveway connected to the association road and also easy access to PVREA powerlines located along the association roadway. This south-facing slope allows for excellent sun exposure to maximize solar gain for the house and to optimize snow melting on the driveway during the winter.

Home Orientation. The home's footprint is 55 feet by 35 feet and is oriented lengthwise along the southern exposure slope to minimize excavation requirements and to take full advantage of solar gain. The house footprint is partially screened from the association roadway by small-sized ponderosa pine trees along the roadway edge. The septic system with a septic tank and sewage disposal field was located in front of the house because there the ground was not as solid and had less rock and more dirt. The septic tank needs to be pumped out annually.

Foundation. The house foundation was poured with attachments for the first floor structurally insulated panels (SIPs) panels. It is very important that the foundation precisely conforms to the blueprint specifications so that the SIPs fit exactly. After the attachments were erected on the foundation supports, the SIPs were attached to one another by metal cams.

Driveway. The path for the driveway connecting the house site with the association road was almost level but required some excavation of hill material. Recycled railroad ties provided support and erosion control on the hillside above the driveway, and the ground was compacted to make a durable and reliable all-weather driveway. A regular size propane tank for home use was located in an indentation of the driveway near the well head and is topped off three times a year. The total cost of the propane use is figured into my average monthly energy cost.

Driveway to home from association road illustrating slope
stabilization with recycled railroad ties and straw wattles

DR. JOHN H. FITCH

Superinsulation. Insulation is essential in a sustainable home. In this home, superinsulation plus a good southern exposure provide sufficient winter heating with roof solar panels and summer cooling to make other sustainable technologies such as solar thermal heating and no air conditioning (as is the case with this home) viable options.

Two types of superinsulation were selected for use in this home: structurally insulated panels and spray foam insulation. Structurally insulated panels (SIPs) are factory-made locally as pre-cut insulated walls that can be load-bearing in many house types. SIPs have tough outside layers of oriented strand board (OSB) and layers of polystyrene insulation of varying thicknesses, depending upon the amount of insulation desired, in the middle. Hardie-board or other external surfaces can be attached to the inside OSB layer making a solid wall capable of bearing a load as an outside wall. Spaces for the electrical wiring can be easily inserted in the SIPs at the factory or on site by sticking heated rebar through the middle insulation materials of the SIPs panels to accommodate the wiring. Using SIPs have several advantages in comparison to the insultation used in conventional stick-built homes including a tighter and better insulated structure, significantly less construction time, and significantly less construction waste on site.

The other type of superinsulation used is a nontoxic spray foam that sets up as a semisolid. It is not load-bearing but is ideal for insulating scissors truss cathedral ceilings and the space between floors. Spray foam is easily applied in required thicknesses for specific insulation values by trained contractors.

I have been very pleased with the performance of both types of insulation. In general, the house walls have R-values of 35-45 and the ceiling has R-values of 65-85. The PVREA has conducted an assessment of my home, including blower door tests, and reported that it is the tightest home they have ever tested.

Electric Grid Tie. In spite of my solar system's ability to produce 10-15% more power than I need, my home is tied to the nearby PVREA power line via a line buried under the driveway and the association roadway. There are several advantages to this arrangement. The grid tie:

- Serves as a large "battery" for home electrical requirements at night;
- Enables the PVREA to purchase excess electrical power from me produced by my solar panels at wholesale rates;
- Enables PVREA power to offset my home's power needs when the solar photovoltaic panels are snow covered for a day or more due to severe snowstorms;
- Makes a reverse mortgage more of a possible option; and,
- Increases house value in the long run.

Solar Photovoltaic System (PV). Solar energy traveling 93 million miles from the sun powers the Earth's biosphere. This energy is used by plants to create chemical energy fuel (carbohydrates) that is the basis of life on Earth. Solar energy is abundant, and scientists have estimated that in two minutes the Earth receives enough solar energy to support all the energy needs of humans on our planet for an entire year! With solar panels, we can capture a portion of that free energy to produce radiant floor heat and to run electric appliances.

My sustainable home showing roof solar hot water panels and solar photovoltaic panels in back yard producing electrical energy

The PV panels are installed on the south-facing slope behind the house. The 20 panels are ground-mounted at an optimal angle to capture sunlight. Solar cells within the panels each contain a semiconductor which, if struck by light energy photons, excites electrons and frees them to circulate and create electric current. The photocells are interconnected within a solar panel so that the flow of electrical current is pooled and then travels toward an inverter that changes direct current (DC) produced by solar cells to alternating current (AC) required to power appliances and lights within the house.

Close up of solar photovoltaic hillside panels producing
10% to 15% more energy than I am using

My home, connected to the PVREA grid, has a net meter that tracks both electricity that is produced by the photovoltaic system and the electricity going from the grid into my system. At night, the PVREA system acts as a large electrical battery for the house. My system also has emergency battery backup provided by lead acid batteries in the photovoltaic shed attached to the house. This emergency system switches automatically to the solar photovoltaic system and battery backup if the outside grid goes down. If the solar photovoltaic system is not functioning properly, the control system switches over automatically to the PVREA grid system only. At night, if the PVREA grid goes down, the system switches automatically to the emergency lead acid batteries that power only the selected emergency circuits.

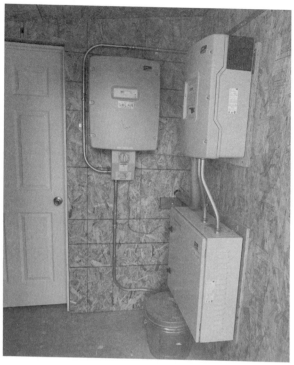

Solar photo voltaic control room integrating current from the solar
panels with alternating current from the commercial power grid

This photovoltaic system produces 5.1 kW with an AC voltage output of 208-240 volts with a DC input voltage of 250-480 volts. Total estimated PV annual AC current production output is 7150 kWh. The system produces approximately 10% to 15% more energy than I actually use. That additional net output is valued by PVREA at wholesale rather than retail rates and is credited to my account over time.

Solar Thermal Radiant Floor Heating System. The solar thermal system is an open-loop, drain-back system with eight roof-mounted 4 ft. by 8 ft. panels in two arrays of four panels each (see photo above of house roof with roof solar panels on page 25). A 1500-gallon insulated solar vault is buried on the northeastern corner of the house with an access hatch in the storage shed above the vault. The solar collection and hot water distribution systems are managed by a proprietary computerized relay controller. The controller manages all water heating equipment in the house including solar hot water collection, domestic hot water heating, and space heating that radiates up through the floor. The controller also has logic and programming controls to switch between the solar heat sources and a backup Munchkin propane boiler to provide heat to any of the loads when it is needed. The controller operates automatically, and no manual input is required, even between seasons! A dedicated computer terminal in the mechanical control room provides access to the MAXMon monitoring software to check the system status and to adjust the sensor temperatures and control logic if necessary.

Control room on first floor showing incoming hot water pipes from solar hot water panels on roof. Incoming hot water from solar panels flows through a heat exchanger and the water then returns to the roof solar panels. The heat exchanger conveys the heat to the 17 different heating zone pipes heating floors in home.

The temperatures of the solar thermal panels and the storage tank are monitored by the solar controller. When the temperature of the solar thermal panels is greater than that of the storage tank by 20 ° F, the solar collector loop pumps are turned on and they run until water in the panels cools to within 4 ° of the storage tank, at which time they are turned off.

In the event that the water in the holding tank is cool and calls for heat, the temperature of the solar panels is checked first. If heat is needed, the heat exchange pump attached to the solar hot water tank is turned on and runs until the desired temperature is achieved. If 30 minutes elapse and the call for heat has still not been satisfied, the solar heat call will be canceled, and the propane boiler will be fired to provide heated water for the domestic hot water storage tank.

In addition to controlling the solar heat collection, the controller also acts as the zone valve controller. All of the thermostats in the 17 different house heating zones are connected to the controller. The controller uses its programed control logic to provide heat to the house using solar heat first and then using the propane boiler as the backup. When a thermostat in the house calls for heat and there is no domestic water call for heat, solar heating will be used if the solar hot water tank is hot enough. If the vault temperature is too cool, the backup propane boiler will be used until the solar hot water tank is heated sufficiently to provide the required hot water.

In addition, an insulated water tank with a capacity of 1500 gallons of water is buried in the backyard to provide auxiliary heat in the winter as well as emergency water to fight forest fires, if necessary.

Why don't the PV panels freeze in cold weather? When solar energy is not available because the panels are covered by snow or the temperature is below freezing, water is automatically drained out of the panels, hence the name "solar thermal drainback system." This drainback system is extremely important because otherwise extensive damage could be done to the PV panels. Also, it is important to realize, is that the water in the panels never comes into direct contact with the hot water that circulates throughout the house. Instead, only the heat, not the water, from the panels passes through a heat exchanger to warm the water circulating through the 17 different heating zones in the home.

Computer control system for radiant floor
heating system throughout the home

Decks. The decking on my home has two functions. The first is to provide a wonderful vantage platform for eating dinners and sleeping outside, and just enjoying beautiful views of Redstone Canyon. Because I sight mountain lions and bears fairly regularly, the deck has been built out from the second level of the house and is only reachable from sturdy sliding glass doors on the second floor. This precaution reduces the number of large uninvited mammals dropping by for dinner!

DR. JOHN H. FITCH

Deck and solar hot water radiant roof panels on
south-facing side of home

The second function of the deck is to provide shade control for the windows in the first-floor solar room during the summer. During the winter, these windows add valuable passive solar heat to the home. The deck floor is made of advanced composite recycled plastic and wood fiber planks that are attached to the deck supports on the bottom of the planks rather than from the top, so as to limit exposure of the attachment points to rain, snow, and ice.

Interior Sustainable Choices

Universal Design. Universal Design refers to the concept that form should follow function and that the layout of the home should satisfy the needs of the homeowners over their life span. The term also refers to installing features that assist people with special needs allowing them to age in place.

My sustainable home is 2300 square feet on two floors. The first floor has a drive-in garage that can accommodate four vehicles as well as my large collection of tools and equipment for fire mitigation. This floor also has an atrium-like solar front hall, an all-purpose room/bedroom with full bath and walk-in shower, mechanical room and two walk-in closets. All rooms are wheelchair accessible. The second floor accommodates a great room with floor-to-ceiling windows that span the canyon and provides views of Pikes Peak (200 miles away), a bedroom and office each with a full bath and walk-in closet, dining area, kitchen, and laundry room. A straight stairway allowing installation of a stairlift connects the two floors.

Four car garage with room for workshop on first floor—note kayaks
hanging from ceiling where they can be easily lowered onto cars

Downstairs solar room fully exposed to winter sun and partially
shielded from summer sun for less sunlight and heat

Upstairs great room showing wonderful southern
exposure, high efficiency woodstove, and view

Kitchen zone of great room on second floor
with view into second floor office

In addition, a dumbwaiter connects the first and second floors so
that groceries can be carried from the garage to the dumbwaiter and
sent up to the second floor. If someone has to be confined to the first
floor by illness or injury, meals prepared in the kitchen on the second
floor can be sent down to the first floor via the dumbwaiter.

Second floor office with heavy sliding glass doors to deck

Second floor bedroom and sliding glass doors to deck

Windows and Doors. The sliding glass doors as well as the windows have double-pane glass and a special film on the inside of the glass. This film allows solar gain when the sun's rays strike the glass directly, as they do in the winter season. When the sun's rays strike the glass more obliquely, as they do in the summer, they are reflected away from the house interior thanks to the film. In addition, every large window and sliding glass door has solar pull-down shades that provide insulation at night during the winter and during the day in the summer.

Paints and Finishes. All interior and exterior paints and finishes that were used were non-toxic except for one exterior paint that was slightly toxic. Floor coverings on the first floor included recycled slate in the solar room. Interface carpet squares made from recycled plastic bottles were installed in the hallways, the downstairs bedroom, and the walk-in closet. Marmoleum, a sustainable floor covering, was installed in all three bathrooms as well as the laundry room. Ash wood floors were laid in the second floor's great room and bedrooms and Interface carpet squares were used in the walk-in closets.

Woodstove. A highly efficient, low-emissions woodstove is located in the great room on the second floor and is useful in supplementing heat on extremely cold nights. It has enough capacity to heat the entire second level of the house, but that has not been necessary to date.

Energy Star Appliances and Lighting. All my electrical appliances are rated as "Energy Star," meaning they are top energy-efficient appliances. All electrical lights in the house use LED bulbs. One of the most cost-effective energy savings measures in homes today is to specify that only LED bulbs should be used for lighting. Not only do they use significantly less electricity, but they have an extended lifetime compared with incandescent bulbs.

In addition, on the second floor, solar tube lights are installed in the laundry room, kitchen, the two bathrooms, and the two walk-in closets.

These solar tubes were developed by NASA for spacecraft lighting and consist of completely enclosed cylinders that conduct solar light from the glass top down to the glass bottom of the tube. Light is conducted down the tube by a series of mirrors and the entire unit is waterproof. These tubes can be as long as six to eight feet so that light can travel from the roof level to the second floor living room, bedroom, bathrooms, office, and kitchen.

Home showing the photovoltaic solar panels and light
tubes on roof that provide light to the second floor

Other Sustainable Choices

Construction Waste. Conventional homes add significantly to already overburdened waste disposal sites used for construction waste. In contrast, by using of SIPs, construction waste from my home was 85% less than would have been produced by a stick-built home. This was not only a financial savings but a sustainable one as well. In addition, all construction zones were graded and replanted with native grasses that were rolled up prior to construction. Straw wattles were used to stabilize slopes and vegetation in erosion-prone areas. The regeneration of native plant species in disturbed areas has been excellent.

Fire Risk. Fires are common in Colorado's Front Range ponderosa forests. In fact, the forest ecology community in this region is referred to as a "ponderosa pine subclimax community," meaning that frequent natural fires keep this ecological community in an intermediate ponderosa pine successional stage. As a protection for my home, lightning rods were installed in strategic positions on the roof as indicated by the builder. Also, fire mitigation cutting of dead trees and branches was done in a fire protection zone around the house.

Fighting wildfires in this region is very challenging because of high winds, deep canyons, and steep terrain. Prescribed burning under controlled conditions can be helpful, but such fires can easily burn out of control. So far, two major forest fires have occurred in the canyon since I built my home. Fortunately, through a combination of good luck and best fire mitigation practices, major damage has been avoided in Redstone Canyon because of these practices.

One practice is to reduce destructive crown fires so they become manageable ground fires and can then be stopped. These fire mitigation methods include the limbing of trees to reduce potential fuel ladders and removal of dense growths of young trees. Second, landowners participate in the Redstone Canyon Fire Mitigation Team which uses fire mitigation treatments strategically in the canyon to reduce fire danger. Our team provides "sweat equity" in cutting and dragging the slash to roadsides. Matching grants from the Colorado Forest Service have made it possible to have the slash chipped and then sprayed back onto the land in an effort to return nutrients to fairly nutrient-poor forest soils. In grassland areas, open-range grazing is permitted in Redstone Canyon to reduce fuel loads.

To date, my sustainable home has not been damaged by wildfires due to a combination of wildfire mitigation practices and good luck.

Chain saw art honoring eagles and mountain lions as well as fire which helps to maintain the ponderosa subclimax ecosystem

Electric Rechargeable Vehicles. The same solar photovoltaic system used to power my home also recharges my electric Polaris Ranger (ATV). This ATV came with lead acid batteries and I worked with a garage in Denver, Colorado to replace them with a lithium battery package which is much more efficient. According to technical information, these batteries should be good for 6,000 recharges. My ATV has a range of some 50 miles in the mountains and runs on one-wheel drive on level ground, two-wheel drive on small inclines, and four-wheel drive in steep areas or when I have a snowblade attached to clear roads. I use it as a work and tour vehicle that makes virtually no noise. I am very pleased with both its power and range, and it is a functioning demonstration that lithium-powered electric ATVs are both cost- and work-effective!

Electric Rechargeable Tools. I do not have to store gasoline in anything but the gas tank of my Toyota 4Runner because all my power tools, including chainsaws, trimmers, mower, blowers, and snow blower, run on rechargeable lithium batteries. Electric lithium-powered chainsaws are safer than gas-powered ones because they are lighter, much quieter, have excellent torque, and can be turned on or off quickly. I use Stihl chainsaws, trimmers, and blowers because of their durability and the interchangeability of batteries among these tools. My lithium batteries have been charged over the last 8 years, and still are just as powerful as they were when new!

My tools including lawn mower, Polaris Ranger ATV and bike all powered by lithium batteries recharged by my photoelectric solar panels (no gasoline needs to be stored!)

Solar-Powered Fence and Gate. Redstone Canyon residents can enroll in an open-range cattle-grazing program during summer and fall months and may fence off up to five acres in the immediate vicinity of their homes to keep the cows away if they wish. I use solar-powered fencing on my property for that purpose. I also have a solar-powered gate at the beginning of the driveway.

Rainwater Harvesting. Rainwater harvesting is now legal in Colorado if your property has a well and the water falling off your roof drains onto your land. I have equipped the house with rainwater-harvesting connections and will be using rainwater harvesting in the future to support food gardens with drip irrigation.

Radon. Another consideration is radon, especially in the mountains. My home was tested when the construction was completed and had extremely low radon levels—well below unsafe concentration levels.

CHAPTER 3

Growing Diversity Of
Sustainable Dwellings

A S DESCRIBED IN CHAPTER 2, the key aspects of sustainable homes are the use of superinsultation, renewable energy resources, and the use of building materials that are nontoxic and long-lived. These characteristics are applicable not only to single family homes but increasingly to a diverse range of dwellings. Although it would be possible to write a book on just the variety of sustainable homes now available, that is beyond the scope of this book. In this chapter, three different examples of sustainable homes are briefly described: tiny homes, sustainable developments including condos, and an older home that can be renovated to be more sustainable.

Sustainable Tiny Homes

Tiny homes have grown out of a need to have housing that is more than a trailer but that can still be mobile. One early type of tiny home grew out of large metal shipping containers that were originally built to ride on the decks of large cargo ships stacked several containers high. Because they were metal, some of these shipping containers were used as guard posts in mountainous areas to interdict illegal arms shipments, drugs, or human trafficking. Another early type of tiny home was the small mobile house trailer that could be transported to different sites as something a step up from tent shelters. Tiny homes have also been used as short-term housing for families having to abandon their homes suddenly as a result of forest fires, flooding, or other types of disasters.

Well insulated "tiny homes" can be very energy efficient and portable as well!

More recently, some "high-end" tiny homes have been designed for people who wish many of the comforts of a home with renewable energy and good insulation, in a very small package that can be towed to a beautiful lake, wildlife preserve, or other place of interest. Well-stocked tiny homes can also be used by researchers conducting ecological studies. Another type of tiny home is a sophisticated trailer or self-propelled vehicle that can serve as a small dwelling with many of the comforts of home for travel or short-term stays in one place. Tiny home approaches have also been used in developing floating tiny homes, some self-propelled, that can be used as temporary accommodations for tourists, sportsmen, and researchers.

There are definitely markets for tiny homes, ranging from those for low income needs to very sustainable and comfortable places for wealthy tourists in unique areas. An emerging opportunity that the City of Denver has been assessing is developing tiny homes that are well-insulated, thus minimizing costs, for low-income housing that is mobile and can be sited where most needed. Another opportunity is to equip tiny homes with solar panels as well as excellent insulation and make them available for communities to use in the aftermath of disasters such as hurricanes and large forest fires. Again, these units are transportable, can supply their own energy, and can help greatly in recovery efforts.

Sustainable Homes/Apartments in Cities

There is definitely a market for sustainable homes, apartments, and apartment buildings in cities and towns. Retirement communities have discovered that sustainable housing units that are well insulated, perhaps with solar or other renewable equipment, are great investments both for individual retirees and as investments for retirement villages. Sustainable homes and apartments are also good investments for universities, hospitals, field research stations, ranches, remote tourist facilities, and military installations. Sustainability planning creates a self-sufficiency of renewable energy resources, weatherization, and recycling programs that may be essential to such communities. Due to low monthly expenses in energy use in addition to lower maintenance costs due to the use of more sustainable building materials, units can have both lower purchase/investment costs as well as significantly lower monthly utilities expenses. Being able to significantly lower purchase/mortgage costs, utility expenses, and upkeep costs will greatly expand opportunities for retirees on fixed incomes as well as students, and individuals or families with low incomes.

Sustainable Community Developments

Sustainable community developments are becoming very popular in progressive towns and cities. Fort Collins, Colorado is a good example of such a community. It has developed an innovative program with its utility providers to transition to 100% renewable energy by the year 2030! Fort Collins and its energy suppliers have developed an innovative program to educate homeowners about renewable energy resources such as solar by developing "solar gardens" within the city. These solar gardens have solar photovoltaic panels in them that citizens can purchase and have their monthly energy bills reduced by the amounts of solar energy produced by their solar panels. This imaginative fully subscribed program gives residents experience with solar energy without having the expense of installing solar panels on the roofs of their homes and is one of the reasons for very strong support among Fort Collins residents for a transition to 100% solar energy by the year 2030.

Fort Collins has another major sustainability advantage, and that is in having Colorado State University (CSU) selected as the most highly-rated sustainable university in the nation, according to the *Princeton Review*. CSU is known for its innovative sustainability practices such as the recycling of waste stream products, use of renewable energy resources, and world wide sustainability education. In addition to CSU's Warner College of Natural Resources and the School of Global Environmental Sustainability, CSU has developed the President's Council on Sustainability Development as well as the Institute for the Built Environment (IBE). The mission of these institutes is to bring students and faculty together with local, regional, national, and international governments and businesses to develop sustainable approaches and technologies for the future. This represents an exceptional opportunity to expand the original concept of a land-grant college into an integrated local and international approach to addressing future sustainability challenges.

Because of its rich and varied sustainable initiatives in local government and higher education, it is no surprise that innovative builders and developers have initiated sustainable community development in the Fort Collins area. As an example, I cite one such sustainable community development, known as REVIVE Properties, in northern Fort Collins which has been awarded the Zero Energy Ready Home EPA Energy Ready Housing Award and the U. S. Department of Energy Housing Innovation Award in 2017. I thank Susan McFaddin (personal communication, 11/12/2019), developer and Realtor, for providing the following information on this development.

REVIVE Properties showing sustainable homes and apartments

REVIVE Properties contains a variety of sustainable
homes, condos, and apartments which use solar and
heat pump energy to greatly lower utility costs

DR. JOHN H. FITCH

One REVIVE homeowner shared the following comments evaluating the Lotus Townhome he purchased:

> *First and foremost, this home is absolutely the nicest place I have ever lived. The building quality is outstanding, far above expectations. There is a substantial economic benefit in going with solar/geothermal heating and cooling. I am making an effort to vote with my wallet about an issue I care about. The move from traditional fuel for home energy is happening, and it will continue to grow using sustainable solar/geothermal heating and cooling.*

This sustainable development is located in an area where there are opportunities for both solar energy and geothermal heating and cooling. First, solar energy can be used for electric generation for heating, cooling, and lighting. Second, because the groundwater level is within heat pump technology range of ground level, geothermal heat pumps can be used to provide thermal heating during the winter and thermal cooling during the summer. For a REVIVE Properties 1,434 square foot 2-bedroom, 2-bath home on three floors, the calculated monthly energy bill would be $20 with an average annual savings estimate of $1,700 and a projected savings over the first 30 years of $72,000. These homes, each with a two-car garage, laundry room, office, kitchen and pantry as well as a patio, range from $305,000 to $325,000 in price. Other larger sustainable developments are being planned in the Fort Collins area because of the popularity of REVIVE Properties.

Sustainable Retrofits of a Conventional Home

I conducted the following interview with Mr. Kevin Cross (personal communication, 1/15/2020), who is a mechanical engineer and has been one of the leaders promoting sustainable planning and building as well as a variety of other renewable energy projects in the Ft. Collins area. His home in the city of Fort Collins Laurel School Historic District is more than 100 years old, having been built in approximately 1899.

I asked him to define the term "sustainability" in relation to retrofitted buildings. He replied that the main U. S. Green Building Council LEED program categories cover the essential points of low energy use, good indoor environmental quality, location with respect to mass transit and other low-impact transport options, use of low-impact materials and resources, low site impact, and low water use, all of which are important components of sustainability for retrofitted buildings.

A beautiful antique home which has been upgraded as a sustainable example of the energy savings possible with older homes

When asked to describe his home before sustainable retrofits in terms of history, age, and unsustainable features, he gave the following information. The house is a two-story structure in which the lower floor is masonry with brick and stucco and no insulation. The second floor is wood framed and was minimally insulated with cellulose in the walls prior to the retrofit. Windows were single-glazed and the house originally had steam heat and no air-conditioning. Small room size and the fact that the living room and kitchen were on the north side of the house meant there was little daylighting for solar energy.

I then asked him to describe the process he used to evaluate and prioritize those aspects of the home in need of sustainable retrofits. He mentioned that he gutted and renovated the home immediately after it was purchased in 1999 to bring it up to modern electrical, structural, and mechanical code requirements. The two floors were opened to make larger rooms in accordance with modern practices. Skylights and an atrium were added to provide more daylighting. A greenhouse was added on the south side of the house, partly to provide heating during the fall and spring seasons. The intent of the renovations was to make the house more energy- and water-efficient and more comfortable than it had been, while preserving its historic character and reusing as many materials as possible.

Although he did not have monthly energy expense information prior to the retrofits above, he described monthly energy expenses after retrofit for the time period between October 2016 and September 2017. Energy use during that period was 2,875 kWh (1.34 kWh/sf) for electricity, 657 therms for gas use, and wood pellet use of 923 pounds for a combined energy use of 0.34 therms per square foot. This equates to an Energy Utilization Index of 38.8 BTU/square foot per year. These figures are very good for a house of this age in our climate. Annual energy expense was $1,032, and with water and sewer included, the annual utility bill was $1,793.

I then asked him to describe the overall impacts of the sustainability retrofits on comfort, interior air quality, and other observations comparing and contrasting the impacts of sustainability retrofits. He mentioned that daylighting, new double-glazed windows on the second floor, storm windows with spring seals on the first floor, generally good sealing of leaks, a hot water heating system, masonry exterior walls on the first floor, and active management of windows and exhaust fans during the summer for cooling have made the house quite comfortable year-round with no air-conditioning needed. The only exception in terms of temperature comfort was when peak ambient temperatures exceeded 90 degrees for several days. After several days of such high temperatures, the second-floor temperatures could reach or exceed 85 degrees F in the late afternoon and early evening.

When asked to describe the materials needed in the retrofits and expertise required for installation, he mentioned that most structural and finish materials including window and door frames, flooring, and cabinetry were retained during the original renovation with the exception of piping and electrical wiring. Insulation was added in the second-floor walls and cathedral ceilings. In addition, windows were replaced on the second floor, and combination storm/screened windows were added on the first floor. Subsequent retrofits added heating pipe insulation, additional insulation and sealing, and a solar hot water system for both domestic hot water and space heating. The original renovation took approximately ten months, and the solar system was subsequently installed in about two months.

In terms of financing, Kevin obtained a state income tax credit for the original renovation because of the historical nature of the house. In addition, he received an incentive payment from the City of Fort Collins for the home insulation and sealing work by a contractor.

Kevin's advice for obtaining technical/construction expertise is to contact your local utilities department for assistance. They may be able to provide a home audit and a list of contractors capable of doing work recommended by the auditor.

CHAPTER 4

How Can Sustainability
Give Us 2020 Vision?

B Y NOW YOU may be wondering why this concept of sustainability is so important. The purpose of this chapter is to delve more deeply into the meaning of sustainability as it applies to our lives and our ability as a species to survive and thrive in the future.

In 1987, in the aftermath of World War II and the continuing Cold War and Space Race, the World Commission on Environment and Development was formed under the leadership of Dr. Gro Brundtland, former Prime Minister of Norway and a world health expert. At the time, astronauts were returning from their explorations with beautiful photographs of the Earth from space, and the international community was beginning to appreciate the Earth as a complex living planet with life that might or might not exist anywhere else in the universe.

The World Commission on Environment and Development in its report, *Our Common Future* (1987), noted the following:

> ...*From space, we can see and study the Earth as an organism whose health depends on the health of all its parts. We have the power to reconcile human affairs with natural laws and to thrive in the process. In this, our cultural and spiritual heritages can reinforce our economic interests and survival imperatives.*

This Commission believes that people can build a future that is more prosperous, more just, and more secure. Our report, **Our Common Future,** *is not a prediction of ever-increasing environmental decay, poverty, and hardship in an ever more polluted world among ever decreasing resources. We see instead the possibility for a new era of economic growth, one that must be based on policies that sustain and expand the environmental resource base* (Our Common Future, p.1).

Humanity can make development sustainable—to ensure that it meets the needs of the present without compromising the ability of future generations to meet their own needs. The concept of the present sustainable development does imply limits—not absolute limits but limitations imposed by the present state of technology and social organizations on environmental resources and by the ability of the biosphere to absorb the effects of human activities (Our Common Future, p.1).

The beautiful color photographs of the Earth taken by astronauts have been a dramatic demonstration that our Earth is, in reality, a "lifeboat" in space. The biosphere of life surrounding the Earth is a fragile, narrow band no wider than 25 miles from the deepest part of the ocean to the highest elevation in the atmosphere where life exists. As we learn more about the other planets in our solar system, we are discovering that some, perhaps including Mars, once had an atmosphere and subsequently lost it. In the case of the Earth, plants help sustain the atmosphere by producing oxygen and taking in carbon dioxide, while animals produce carbon dioxide while taking in oxygen. The Earth's atmosphere includes other gases as well such as nitrogen. The

Earth's atmosphere is helping to sustain a balance of temperatures in the biosphere necessary to maintain life as we know it. If our stable biosphere atmosphere were not present, temperatures on Earth could vary from 500 degrees F during the day to minus 200 degrees F at night!

We know, based on scientific evidence, that the Earth's atmosphere goes through gradual changes over time based on a variety of factors such as volcanic activity and sea level change, and that those factors have led to periodic ice ages and interglacial warming periods. With the current universal use of fossil fuels as an energy source on Earth, the levels of carbon dioxide and other greenhouse gases have risen rapidly enough to induce unintended climate changes. The rapidity of these human-induced climate changes is causing concerns because of the threat of sea level rise as glacial ice melts, and because of the impacts of drier, hotter conditions in some key agricultural areas. Significant sea level rise is already threatening some U.S. cities, several islands, and other nations. Current predictions are that sea level rise in the next 100 years could threaten large coastal cities in many nations where a significant percentage of the Earth's human population resides.

As stated by the World Commission on Environment and Development, our challenge at this point is to ensure that our use of energy and other aspects of future development *"meet the needs of the present generation without compromising the ability of future generations to meet their own needs(emphasis added)."* Although the conventional building industry has depended upon inexpensive fossil fuels for heating and cooling of both residential and commercial buildings, continuing dependence solely on fossil fuels is not a sustainable solution for future generations. Fortunately, there are two sustainable approaches that are currently available for present and future generations: improved insulation and renewable energy from geothermal, solar, and wind sources.

The good news is that sustainable building techniques and materials are available now that not only drastically reduce or eliminate fossil fuel use, but also improve building air quality, reduce maintenance expenses, and extend the useful lives of buildings. And the costs of these techniques and materials are competitive or even less than presently used conventional techniques. Sustainable building techniques and materials are designed to meet the needs of the present generation without compromising the ability of future generations to meet their own needs. Our major challenge is integrating economic sustainability, environmental sustainability, and societal/sociopolitical sustainability on an intergenerational basis.

If we consider our economy, environment, and society as overlapping systems of life, we can understand both the importance and the responsibility of our species to integrate and sustain a balance among them. All three systems are integral to our planet's health; the whole is only as healthy as the sum of its parts as illustrated in Figure 1.

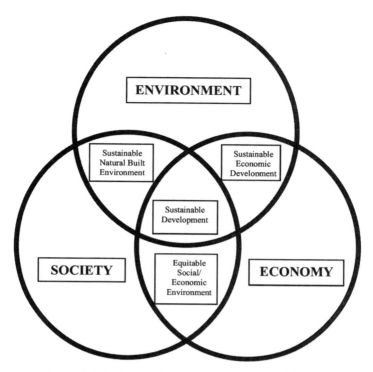

Figure 1. The integral parts of our sustainable planet

As an example of this concept, we can learn much from indigenous cultures that are more familiar with natural environments and their limits than is our own. Many of the Great Plains Native American tribes depended upon bison not only for food, shelter, and clothing, but also for the role they played in Native spiritual life. Bison were an essential part of the Great Plains ecosystem of life. When the bison were decimated by widespread hunting and the policies of the U. S. Army, it led to subjugation of Plains tribes. Thus, when one of the three circles is denied a critical resource, the results can be catastrophic. Perhaps we have finally learned a lesson, because lately there has been much interest in bringing back bison to the Great Plains. They are well adapted for that ecosystem and for sustaining it. They are able to adjust to harsh winter conditions and to predators they might encounter, and their hides and meat are in demand. However, damage to the Great Plains Native American tribes was permanent.

The concept of sustainability also gives us an understanding of natural ecosystems, in which native plants and animals interact with specific soils and climates to be completely self-supporting. Ecologists have learned much about the ways in which sunlight energy, photosynthesis, and energy flow from plants, to plant-eaters, to eaters of plant-eaters, and to the bacteria and fungi that break down and recycle these nutrients for future generations. There are specialized ecosystems for every climate on Earth, and we can learn much from their amazing complexity, efficiency, and ability to adjust to different conditions.

In Redstone Canyon, I am surrounded by native ecosystems that are balanced by climate, geology, soils, native vegetation, and soil nutrients. The contrast between life here in Redstone Canyon and life in a city is captured by the following hilarious, fictitious conversation between God and St. Francis called *God and Lawn Care.*

God to St. Francis	*St. Francis, you know all about gardens and nature. What in the world is going on down there on the planet? What happened to the dandelions, violets, milkweeds and stuff I started eons ago? I had a perfect no-maintenance garden plan. Those plants grow in any type of soil, withstand drought and multiply with abandon. The nectar from long-lasting blossoms attracts butterflies, honey bees, and flocks of songbirds. I expected to see a vast garden of colors by now. But, all I see are these green rectangles!*
St. Francis to God	*It's the tribes that settled down there, Lord, the Suburbanites! They started calling your flowers "weeds" and went to great lengths to kill them and replace them with grass!*

God to St. Francis	*Grass? But it is so boring! It's not colorful. It doesn't attract butterflies, birds, bees—only grubs and sod worms. It's sensitive to temperatures. Do these Suburbanites really want all that grass growing there?*
St. Francis to God	*Apparently so, Lord! They go to great pains to grow it and keep it green. They begin each spring by fertilizing the grass and poisoning any other plant that crops up in the lawn!*
God to St. Francis	*The Spring rains and warm weather probably make the grass grow really fast! That must make the Suburbanites happy.*
St. Francis to God	*Apparently not, Lord. As soon as it grows a little, they cut it, sometimes twice a week!*
God to St. Francis	*They cut it? Do they bale it like hay?*
St. Francis to God	*Not exactly, Lord. Most of them rake it up and put it in bags.*
God to St. Francis	*They bag it? Why? Is it a cash crop? Do they sell it?*
St. Francis to God	*No Sir, just the opposite. They pay to throw it away!*
God to St. Francis	*Now, let me get this straight! They fertilize grass so it will grow. And when it does grow, they cut it off and pay to throw it away*
St. Francis to God	*Yes, Sir.*
God to St. Francis	*These Suburbanites must be relieved in the summer when we cut back on the rain and turn up the heat. That surely slows the growth and saves them a lot of work.*
St. Francis to God	*You aren't going to believe this, Lord. When the grass stops growing so fast, they drag out hoses and pay more money to water it, so they can continue to mow it and pay to get rid of it!*

God to St. Francis	*What nonsense! At least they kept some of the trees. That was a sheer stroke of genius, if I do say so myself. The trees grow leaves in the spring to provide beauty and shade in the summer. In the autumn, they fall to the ground and form a natural blanket to keep moisture in the soil and protect the trees and bushes. It's a natural cycle of life*
St. Francis to God	*You had better sit down, Lord! The Suburbanites have drawn a new circle. As soon as the leaves fall, they rake them into great piles and pay to have them hauled away!*
God to St. Francis	*No! What do they do to protect the shrub and tree roots in the winter to keep the soil moist and loose?*
St. Francis to God	*After throwing away the leaves, they go out and buy something which they call mulch. They haul it home and spread it around in place of the leaves*
God to St. Francis	*And where do they get this mulch?*
St. Francis to God	*They cut down trees and grind them up to make mulch!*
God to St. Francis	*Enough! I don't want to think about it anymore! St. Catherine, you're in charge of the arts. What movie have you scheduled for us tonight?*
St. Catherine to God	*"Dumb and Dumber," Lord. It is a story about…*
God to St. Catherine	*Never mind! I think I just heard the whole story from St. Francis!*

Needless to say, this fictitious interchange points up the contrast between the native ecosystems that surround me with their beauty and diversity at no cost, and hybrid grass yards in cities.

I have wonderful native grasses around the home and trim them every so often with my rechargeable lithium battery-powered lawn mower. Deer frequently graze in my front and back yards. Birds nest in trees near the house and rabbits also help to trim the grass. Thus, my annual budget for natural yard maintenance is nonexistent because I live within the natural ecosystem that surrounds me!

CHAPTER 5

Sustaining Tomorrow Today

O UR SPECIES HAS made tremendous strides in technologies and methods that provide energy, insulation, heating, cooling, and mass construction of homes. However, there is increasing evidence that many of the technologies and methods developed in building and powering conventional homes come at unsustainable costs to our health, economy, and environment, now and in the future. For example, past technologies for heating and cooling homes require the mass extraction and extensive use of fossil fuels including coal, oil, and gas as well as nuclear plants in some cases. Extensive dependence on the mining and use of fossil fuels is already causing changes in climate, including more destructive storms and hurricanes as well as the melting of glaciers leading to sea level rise.

Dependence on nonrenewable energy might be required if no other alternatives were available, but renewable energies are now available that are less expensive even if the costs of extracting non-renewable energies are not included in the equation! And it is important to realize that those extraction costs are real for non-renewal energies; in many cases they involve environmental and even geopolitical expenses, and they are limited in supply and thus are not renewable.

By contrast, renewable energy with today's technologies is easily available and practical to obtain and use. (I like to say my principal renewable energy supplier is located 93 million miles away and has been supplying energy to Earth with great reliability for the last 4.5 billion years.) On the other hand, some proponents of using outdated coal plants assert that these plants should continue in service. Otherwise, they become "abandoned economic resources." This argument ignores the fact that their costs in terms of pollution far outweigh their benefits. The sun is the true "abandoned economic resource" if it is not used. Just a few minutes of sunlight, if we could collect all of it, would meet all of our energy needs on Earth for an entire year!

Fortunately, more nations, states, businesses, and individual homeowners are realizing that renewable energies provided by solar and wind are not only cost-effective but environmentally much safer as well. Complex and somewhat vulnerable power grids are becoming more localized and easier to sabotage. Energy experts from Ukraine, while visiting my home, mentioned that several hundred people were dying in their homes every year during the winter because of Russian sabotage of their electric grids.

Energy independence is another advantage because, today, individual homeowners can harvest their own energy. As mentioned earlier, I am grid-connected, some of which I sell back to the grid, but I also harvest solar heat for radiant floor heating in the house. All my electric tools are powered by lithium batteries as is my Polaris Ranger ATV. Maintenance costs are much lower than for gas-powered tools and my electric tools are still going strong after eight years of hard use. Also, if the grid power goes down, I will still have power because of my photovoltaic collector along with backup batteries. Thus, there is never a question of whether my garage doors will open, which was a problem in California where the electric grid had to be shut down.

California deserves great credit for having the courage to pass legislation requiring that all new houses without major shade install solar panels on their roofs! And I also celebrate President Carter for his wonderful gift to Plains, Georgia of solar panels that will meet 50% of the energy needs of the entire town! In a nutshell, I believe that renewable energy technologies can give this great country energy dependence while reducing energy costs for households! Another benefit is that families, towns, cities, and countries can all achieve energy independence without the costs and/or complications of pollution, foreign supplies that can be cut off, or grid failures due to storms or sabotage. To me, there is a wonderful feeling of freedom in knowing that I have both a sustainable home and energy independence! Even in a good storm with high wind and with the grid down due to tree fall, I know that I will have energy and communications capacity.

I am pleased to report that sustainable building is becoming increasingly available and, I believe, represents one of the best investments available. You can count on not only saving money but also on having a home that is more comfortable and healthy as well as being a better investment. To make it even more attractive, you will be using renewable energy resources that cause no air pollution!

However, for a sustainable future, we must think beyond our own homes. In the final analysis, we need to maintain a global balance between the three circles of sustainability: economic, environmental and societal/cultural. In considering issues and planning for the future, it is imperative that these three domains not only touch one another but overlap as much as possible as shown in Figure 1 on page 59.

It may be helpful to consider a fairly simple example from everyday life. Consider driving a car under different road and weather conditions. Assuming a sober driver, he or she must be aware of the car's speed, the weather, road conditions, and traffic. This driver has to consider all these variables independent of one another, and also integrate them by deciding how they affect one another. Good driver judgement depends on the ability to understand how these variables interrelate and influence one another. Driving on snow and ice versus dry pavement completely changes the driving patterns of experienced drivers who are able to simultaneously integrate complex conditions.

Achieving sustainability will call for a similar type of thinking. Let us say, for example, that we make a major investment in nonrenewable energy such as coal or natural gas that over time has hidden pollution costs that contribute to the degradation of the environment and also impact human well-being. These problems will, in turn, negatively affect economic innovation and growth. These problems inevitably will result in a downward spiral of global well-being unless these cause-effect conditions are integrated in our thinking and interrupted in practice.

By contrast, let us presume we develop technologies that allow us to harvest renewable energy such as sunlight for solar electrical energy and wind for wind electrical energy. Harvests of such renewable energies cause little pollution, are easily obtained without major economic extractive expenses, and are renewable in the sense that their supply is endless. If we make a major investment in renewable energy such as sun or wind, then over time, our environmental problems will decrease, and human health and well-being will improve, and vigorous economic development will occur. If you believe in wise economic investments, which energy resources would you choose?

Our challenge is to develop both short- and long-term strategies that integrate our economic, environmental and societal needs to the greatest extent possible. In doing so, we will be moving forward to a sustainable future rather than speeding ahead on ice! I believe it is possible to develop a sustainable future where renewable energy alternatives, along with the increasing efficiency of insulation, sustainable agricultural practices, and renewable harvesting, will lead to intergenerational equity among cultures and societies.

The goal in such projections for a sustainable future is that the wealth of a society, including the social capital of its cultures, the knowledge capital of economics and sustainable technologies, and the natural environmental capital should not decline (Arrow et al., 2004). Such a system of economic, environmental, and societal sustainability could eventually reach a "golden-rule" integrative state (Endress et al., 2005) with cultural and environmental interlinkages, intergenerational equity through time, and dynamic efficiency (Stavins et al., 2003). The triple bottom line leading to global sustainability becomes the simultaneous and sustainable advancement of economic prosperity, environmental quality, and social equity among different ecosystems and cultures (Hasna, 2007). The good news is that a sustainable future is possible for the human species, the Earth's natural living environment, and an equitable economy as long as our human species realizes that a sustainable future can only be maintained through cultural and environmental interlinkages, intergenerational equity, and the restoration and conservation of vital natural ecosystems of the Earth.

I have the wonderful opportunity to live in a sustainable home in the semi-natural ponderosa and grassland ecosystem of beautiful Redstone Canyon. The experience of living up here has taught me that a sustainable future is indeed possible because of the reliability of environmental technologies, the economic savings that accrue with such technologies, and the health and dependability of renewable energies. In addition, the natural beauty of this canyon and its wildlife diversity have given me a quality of life that I never imagined possible! All this in time to celebrate the 50th anniversary of Earth Day this year with 2020 vision!

Although we have much potential for the future, still with us are the old and all-too-familiar "night riders" of rapid climate change, widespread crop failures, starvation, disease, crime, and war. Worse, the rapid loss of our humanity could imperil the very existence of our species and the millions of other innocent species caught in the vortex of this great whirlpool-like catastrophe. The supreme irony at this point in time is that our species has understood and even predicted the reasons for our own demise, as well as the extinctions of other species, and yet has lacked the collective intelligence, will, resolve, and courage to work cooperatively to avoid this tragedy of global and cosmic proportions.

We still have time to script a different ending if we can cast aside our hubris and begin resolving petty political and power quarrels. We do have both the ability and the moral imperative to turn the approaching tide of global destruction into a spring tide that renews and sustains the Earth's biosphere rather than draining it into a lifeless planet. This effort will require profound and visionary cooperation and leadership locally, regionally, nationally, and globally but we have an example to follow in this country!

During the first Earth Day a half-century ago, the U.S. Congress came together to produce the "Magna Carta" of sustainability legislation. To accomplish this life-giving transfusion for our imperiled species and planet again, let us follow that earlier example of bipartisan courage, to designate this decade as "The 2020 Restoration and Renewal of Our Earth's Life for a Sustainable Future." This truly must be our global defining moment and legacy as a species because, having inserted ourselves into the evolutionary process of life, we have a special responsibility to renew and sustain life-giving processes on planet Earth. We must realize, teach, and inspire a sense that the sustainable elements of ecology, economics, and society are not opposing forces but rather are constructive and interactive powers that must work together to restore, renew, and sustain life, as the Brundtland Commission recommended 32 years ago. But, unlike the situation at that time, we now have the sustainability technologies as well as the understanding to restore, renew, and sustain our species, other life, and our planet for the future!

Let us take a moment this Earth Day to realize that a sustainable future is possible, practical, and like the first Earth Day, requires the best ideas and efforts of all of us working together. With that cooperation, we can sustain our own lives, our economic and social future, and the lives and future of other species that join us on this beautiful and living Earth.

ACKNOWLEDGEMENTS

WHEN I WAS seven years old, my father, Henry S. Fitch, set me on a useful and rewarding track when I went to his office and proudly proclaimed I was going to write the history of the world as my life's work. My father took down a book from his library shelf entitled *The Outline of History* by H. G. Wells and said gently it had already been done! This was a moment of despair for me until he said something else which has been a lifelong gift! He said, "the history the world may have been written but it always needs updating. And even more important, if you write about the future of the world you will always have new material." It was my mother, Virginia R. Fitch, who gave me an appreciation of culture and society, as well as the knowledge that life, even though not perfect, is always something we work together to make better.

This book is about working together to "sustain tomorrow today" by creating homes that sustain our lives, economy, and the Earth. Many people, including former President Jimmy Carter, have encouraged my work and helped me see that a sustainable future is possible. Others who have given me valuable perspectives in this work include Amory Lovins, David Orr, and Brian Dunbar. Professor Dunbar helped by inviting me to work with him in the CSU Graduate Course in Sustainable Technology which set the stage for the planning and construction of my sustainable home in Redstone Canyon. Lee Barker was my primary builder and his dedication, despite personal losses in the High Plains Fire, was extremely helpful especially in the planning, budgeting, and coordinating the building efforts. Tommy Harris of T.

Harris Construction was an extraordinary asset in the magic of getting construction right on site as well as coming up with new ideas and solving problems. His "can do" attitude and honesty were essential in this project. Custom Solar Company of Boulder was extremely helpful in getting the hot water solar roof panels and photovoltaic hillside panels operating correctly. In general, Northern Colorado was a great place to build a sustainable home where I found excellent support in terms of building materials, sustainable technologies equipment and supplies, as well as technical advice and trouble shooting. Access to knowledgeable suppliers and installers in Fort Collins, Loveland, and Boulder made the construction of my sustainable home easy.

I also want to thank Brian Propp for his continuing friendship, considerable expertise in building with structurally insulated panels (SIPS), and his excellent advice on a variety of issues. Colorado State University Deans Patrick Burns of Morgan Libraries and John P. Hayes of Warner College of Natural Resources were also helpful in providing me with an academic home as an affiliate full professor in both Morgan Libraries and the Warner College of Natural Resources Department of Ecosystem Science and Sustainability. Alex Curry was the paid photographer on the project and did an excellent of photo documentation. He used a drone to capture the placement of my sustainable home in the Canyon.

I decided it was imperative to get this book out prior to the 50th anniversary of Earth Day in late April, 2020. This goal would have been impossible without the editorial and production assistance of my special friend Dr. Catherine Alter. Catherine with her strong academic background, excellent editorial skills, and amazing patience has helped me meet a very short deadline. In working with Xlibris Publishing Company, due to the short timeline, I have greatly appreciated the help, encouragement and coordination of Ms. Milane Ramirez.

In addition, I very much appreciate the excellent advice and counsel of Al Billington, Matt Blair, and Kevin Cross as readers and advisors. Ms. Arion Enyart gave me excellent advice about Xlibris Publishing Company and Attorney Michael D. Liggett was most helpful in developing an agreement with Xlibris.

REFERENCES

Allen, J. (2015). *Home: How Habitat Made Us Human*. New York, NY: Basic Books.

Arrow, K. J., Dasgupta, P., Goulder, G., Daily, P.R., Ehrlich, G.M., Heal, S. and B Walker (2004). Are We Consuming Too Much? *Journal of Economic Perspectives*, 18(3): 147-172.

Barnett, D. L. & Browning, W.D. (1995). *A Primer on Sustainable Building*. Boulder, CO: Rocky Mt. Institute.

Boyle, Godrey (Ed.) (2004). *Renewable Energy: Power for A Sustainable Future* (2nd Edition). Oxford, England: Oxford University Press.

Chiras, D. D. (2004). *The New Ecological Home*. White River Junction, VT: Chelsea Green Publishing Company.

Chiras, D. D. (2002). *The Solar House: Passive Heating and Cooling*. White River Junction, VT: Chelsea Green Publishing Company.

Daly, H. E. (1973). *Towards a Steady State Economy*. San Francisco, CA: W.H. Freeman.

Dean, A. M. (2003). *Green by Design: Creating a Home for Sustainable Living*. Layton, UT: Gibbs Smith.

Endress, L.H., Roumasset, J.A. & Zhou. T. (2005). Sustainable Growth with Environmental Spillovers. *Journal of Economic Behavior and Organization*. 58(4): 527-547.

Great Spirit Prayer. Retrieved 1.27.2020 from https://aktalakota.stjo.org/site/news

Hasna, A. M. (2007). Dimensions of Sustainability. *Journal of Engineering for Sustainable Development: Energy, Environment, and Health.* 2 (1): 47-57.

Kaufman, M. & Remick, K. (2009). *Prefab Green.* Layton, UT: Gibbs Smith Publishers.

Koones, S. (2010). *Prefabulous and Sustainable: Building and Customizing an Affordable Energy Efficient Home.* New York, NY: Abrams Books.

Kruger, A. & Seville, C.. (2013). *Green Building: Principles and Practices in Residential Construction.* Boston, MA: Cengage Learning.

Mendler, S. F., & William, O. (2000). Hoboken, New Jersey: John Wiley and Sons.

Mobbs, M. (1998). *Sustainable House: Living for Our Future.* Harrisonburg, VA: Choice Books.

Orr, D. W. (2020). *The Nature of Design: Ecology, Culture, and Human Intention.* Oxford, England: Oxford University Press.

Pearson, D. (2005). *Designing Your Natural Home: A Practical Guide.* New York, NY: Collins Design, Imprint of Harper Collins Publishers.

Ritter, Jr., B. (2016). *Powering Forward.* Boulder, CO: Fulcrum Publishing.

Roaf, S., Fuentes, M., & Thomas, S. (2001). Hudson, NY: Architectural Press.

Rocky Mountain Institute Green Development Services (1995). *A Primer on Sustainable Building.* Boulder, CO: Rocky Mt. Institute.

Van Der Ryn, S., & Cowan, S. (1996). *Ecological Design: Tenth Anniversary Edition.* Washington, DC: Island Press.

Massachusetts Audubon Society (1982). *The Energy Saver's Handbook for Town and City People.* Emmaus, PA: Rodale Press.

The World Commission on Environment and Development (1987). *Our Common Future.* New York, NY: Oxford University Press.

Susanka, S. & Vassallo, M. (2005). *Inside the Not So Big House.* Newton, CN: The Taunton Press.

Stavins, R. N., Wagner, A.F., & Wagner, G.(2003). Interpreting Sustainability in Economic Terms: Dynamic Efficiency Plus Intergenerational Equity. *Economics Letters*, 79 (2003): 339–343.

Venolia, C., & Kelly L. (2006). *Natural Remodeling for the Not-So-Green House.* Asheville, NC: Lark Books.

Wilson, A., & Piepkorn, M. (Eds.) (2008). *Green Building Products 3rd Edition: The GreenSpec Guide to Residential Building Materials.* Gabriola Island, BC Canada: New Society Publishers New.

INDEX

ABOUT THE AUTHOR

*D*R. JOHN H. *Fitch* has studied and written about ecosystems conservation, animal behavior, environmental policy, and sustainability for 55 years. He received his BA in anthropology and zoology from the University of Kansas and an MS and Ph. D in ecology and animal behavior from Michigan State University. He has served on the faculties of Michigan State University, Tufts, Florida Gulf Coast University, and Colorado State University; in leadership positions with several nonprofits including the Massachusetts Audubon Society, Mainewatch Institute, and The Conservancy of Southwest Florida. He also worked as a scientist and assistant field director with Smithsonian Institution on biological surveys of the Central South Pacific Ocean.

As a Faculty Fellow in the Carter Administration, he witnessed solar panels being installed on the White House and became committed to sustainability. He saw the potential of renewable solar and wind energies and superinsulation as a means to decrease dependency on more expensive and potentially polluting nonrenewable energies. His special interest in renewable and sustainable futures on state, national, and international levels led to his slogan: "together we can sustain tomorrow today!" To demonstrate what he advocates, he had built a sustainable demonstration home in beautiful Redstone Canyon near Ft. Collins, Colorado, which he describes in his book, Creating Homes That Can Sustain Our Lives, Economy, and the Earth.

Currently, he serves as an affiliate Full Professor at Colorado State University in the Warner College of Natural Resources Department of Ecosystem Science and Sustainability and in Morgan Libraries. He continues to enjoy his lovely sustainable home in Redstone Canyon, Colorado and has welcomed more than 600 people including CSU students to tour his sustainable home and conservation lands.